Student life in the UK

A guide for international students

By Agnieszka Karch

Contents

Preface

Well done! If you're reading this book, it's highly likely that you've already made up your mind about coming to study in the UK. Or at least, you're seriously considering this option. That's why I'm saying 'well done' – you will certainly not regret it. Studying in the UK was a great educational, developmental and cultural opportunity for me, and I'm sure you will, at least to a certain degree, share this view once you've graduated in a few years' time.

Anyway, the point of this book is not to convince you that British universities are worth your time and money. You have almost certainly already done your research into the quality of education they provide, the content of the courses they offer, and the general financial and practical implications of studying in the UK. The point of this book is to tell you about all the other things that come with this educational experience. All the little things that you couldn't possibly know because you've never been a student before, and certainly – you've never been a student in the UK!

Before coming to the UK to study, I thought I already had a good idea of what to expect. I, like you – I'm sure, had studied English, met some British people in my country and abroad, watched Monty Python and Fawlty Towers and so on, and so on.

When I was accepted for my BA in English Literature and French, I received my university's international student's guide. I flicked through it and thought: seen it all before! I thought it was all common sense. OK, not everything – I hadn't realised that the fact that it's raining is

5

not a good enough excuse for a British person to stay in! And believe me – it's not. Since I moved to the UK, I have grown totally immune to rain. I don't mind it – in fact, I quite like it sometimes! But apart from this little curiosity, I didn't learn that many new things from the guide provided by my university. I thought the main reason for this was that I was coming from a European country. I thought European countries must all be pretty much the same. I had visited a number of them before so I thought I had quite a good understanding of what life was generally like in those countries.

That's right – generally. To tell you the truth, upon my arrival in the UK, I realised that being a tourist in a country for a week or two doesn't equal to getting to know the country and its people at all! I was gobsmacked!

So, if you want to be at least a little bit more prepared than I was when I arrived in the UK to start my university degree, continue reading and you may decide to take some of my tips to heart!

I've organised this book alphabetically, into dictionary-like entries. If you feel that you know about some things more than others, feel free to skip those all too familiar sections and pick the ones you think you don't know too much about. There's no particular order in which you should read this book either, so don't worry if you fancy starting from the end and making your way back to the beginning!

For further information about studying in the UK, including videos with learning tips, have a look at my blog:

www.ukstudentlifeguide.wordpress.com

Accents

One thing that you will certainly notice in your first week at university is that each person has a different one. What? Accent! OK, this is a bit of an exaggeration. Not everyone speaks with a different accent but it might seem that way at the start.

In Poland, which is where I originally come from, we never used to get many British TV shows on telly. Monty Python and Fawlty Towers were probably exceptions. All the other foreign ones were in the vast majority American. American English was therefore what I, and most people in my country, were most familiar with. British English was a rare luxury that your ears would be exposed to if you happened to run into an English tourist visiting your city or went to an English language school for conversation classes with a so-called 'native speaker'. Otherwise, American English was the one variety of English that I was ever exposed to.

As a result, I had a vague idea that there was something called Queen's English and then there was a northern accent. But that was pretty much it! Imagine my surprise when, in the first couple of days in Sheffield, I spoke to people from Newcastle, York and Wales and none of them sounded like anything I'd learned back home. And then there were the Scottish people whose accent, compared to the American English that I had been trained in, was an even greater novelty to me!

Don't be afraid to ask

One thing that I didn't know is that native English speakers can actually hear those accents too. It wasn't just me. British people can in fact figure out that someone is from Bristol or London, or the Midlands. I still can't tell, after so many years in this country. OK, I can tell London, Manchester and Liverpool. It takes so much practice and travelling around to be able to distinguish between them.

As I said, British people are better trained than us, international students, at distinguishing between accents. And they do know that we, international students, may have some trouble not only recognising accents but also understanding them. Make no mistake – Geordie, Scouse, Brummie and Cockney don't sound anything like what you hear on American telly.

And then there's the glottal stop. The 't's disappearing in the middle and at the end of words. That's where things get confusing, as it's quite hard to figure out whether somebody's talking about a play or a plate, or saying that something is great or grey.

My tip here would be: don't be afraid to ask questions. The first type of question you might want to ask is whether they can repeat what they've just said. There's nothing embarrassing about asking people to say something again.

Personally, I was embarrassed to ask, which meant that for the first two months of my stay I laughed at some jokes that weren't funny, agreed with statements that I would have never agreed with, had I understood what was being said, and was up for going to places without knowing where I was going. And believe me – it's not worth it. It's less embarrassing to ask than to agree or nod to things that you're not keen on. You don't want to be taken for a person that you're not, do you?

Anyway, most people will be impressed that you can speak good English. Therefore, they won't mind making things a bit easier for a genius like yourself by repeating what they've just said.

Secondly, don't be afraid to ask people about their accents. They'll be happy to tell you where they're from, and will be up for having a chat about their native tongue. Many people take their native language for granted and hardly ever challenge themselves on why they say things the way they do. Think about your own native language – do you ever question why you pronounce certain words the way you do? Or do you just say them? If you're like most people who use language, it's probably the latter. Many British people I have met have been excited or intrigued about exploring their own language because it's something they had never done before. So, ask people about their accents if you're unsure – there's so much knowledge about and appreciation for the English language that you (and they) can gain from it.

Accommodation

One of the biggest questions you might be asking yourself when thinking about studying in the UK is: where am I going to live? This is exactly the question I was asking myself and, having experienced student life already, I can assure you – there are plenty of options, so don't panic!

Option one is university accommodation. Your university will certainly provide you with lots of information on it and it might even recommend that you stay in its own accommodation. That's what universities do. They own lots of different types of accommodation – big halls of residence (catered or self-catered), flats, and so on. These are very easy to arrange. You usually apply to stay there once you've been accepted on your course.

Many universities guarantee university accommodation for first-year students, but not after that. Don't worry, though – you will certainly have found potential flatmates for your second year by the end of your first year.

Option two is privately rented accommodation. It basically means a flat, which you normally share with other students. This is also fine, especially if you're on a tight budget. Renting privately can, in many cities around the UK, be cheaper than going for university-owned accommodation.

If you do decide to opt for private accommodation, there are a couple of things to remember. Most universities will be able to provide you with a list of landlords who are registered with the university. This basically means that in case anything goes wrong, you can get your uni's support when sorting it out. Not that it will, but this guarantee will give you some extra peace of mind.

The other thing to remember is that renting a flat in your first year is different than staying in university accommodation. It's more like being an adult. It's independent. There's nobody telling you what to do and what time you should have your evening meal. However, it's also not the same in that you're not staying with lots of other students 24/7. This might be a consideration for you, but remember that your university will have a wide social offer anyway, so no matter which option you choose, you won't be missing out on any student fun!

Bank holiday

This isn't exactly a holiday for those who work in banks. Well, technically it is. But not just for them. On bank holidays, most people get a day off work. Your university lecturers do too. And so do you! There are several bank holidays throughout the year so make sure you know when they are in case you turn up for a 9 a.m. class in vain!

Remember that many shops will be closed too, and public transport might be running a reduced service. Stock up on food and plan what you're going to do and how you're going to get around to avoid disappointment!

Bikes

Many people in the UK, including students, ride their bikes. They cycle to get some exercise but also to get from A to B. Cycling is also an environmentally friendly means of transport, which appeals to many people. Most students can't afford a car anyway – so it's a cheap alternative as well!

Some cities are better at providing a safe environment for cyclists than others. This will really vary so make sure you do your own research if you're considering cycling in your university town. In London, for example, it is highly recommended to wear a helmet and fluorescent clothing. In smaller towns, there may be traffic-free zones where cyclists are allowed, which makes riding your bike much safer.

And finally, if you decide to get a bike and use it, make sure you lock it up properly, especially if you're going to study in a big city, such as London. You will see some heavy chains around, which might seem a bit over the top, but it's better to be safe than sorry!

Buses

Buses in the UK don't always stop at every bus stop. This is a very important detail to remember if you ever want to get anywhere.

To get on a bus, you will need to stick your hand out to let the driver know this. Similarly, you will need to press a 'stop' button inside the bus if you want to get off. Otherwise, the driver won't know and you'll end up far, far away.

Also, remember to buy your ticket from the driver when you get on. Different rules apply in different cities but this is a general rule which is true in most of them. You will not be able to sneak on unnoticed.

Careers service

This is something that many students don't fully understand. Or perhaps they don't take interest in finding out what the careers service is all about. This was certainly the case when I went to university.

Many of my friends didn't really know that a careers service existed at our university when they were in their first year. Neither did I! Or maybe we just didn't care. We probably thought that we were too young to bother, and none of us really thought we would ever actually have a career! This is partly fair enough – you want to have fun whilst you can, do fun things like going out most nights and staying in bed all Sunday. However, it might not be the best choice to completely ignore the future ahead of you.

You need a balance of things. You should have as much fun as you reasonably need, but balance it out by occasionally thinking about and doing serious things. One of those things could be visiting your university careers service and finding out what jobs there are out there and what experience you may need to apply for them once you've graduated. They will also be able to help you write your CV, give you advice on how to keep it up to date, and they may even be able to arrange for you to have a practice interview with their specialist advisers.

Even though having a job seems like a distant prospect when you first start university, you're not losing anything by taking some small steps that can result in a head start later on!

Counselling

If you're feeling homesick or generally down for any reason whatsoever, you may be able to use the counselling services which are provided by most universities. This usually involves a one-to-one appointment with a counsellor who will have lots of experience helping students struggling with various issues during their university time. They will be able to give you advice and provide you with support. It's also worth remembering that your conversations will be kept confidential.

Course reps

Course reps, or course representatives, are people elected or appointed to represent the students within their department. There might be reps who represent a whole department or just an individual year group. Course reps are supposed to connect with the student body, listen to its views and pick up any issues that come up. They are then expected to take these to the department authorities and try and work out a solution that works for everyone.

It might be a good idea to consider applying for a course rep role as and when one comes up. It's a great experience to put on your CV and a very rewarding role. You will meet new people, including other reps and members of staff, and get to hear all the gossip before everyone else!

Discounts

Students in the UK can benefit from a number of discounts, which you will probably already know because most countries in the world offer special deals to the lucky holders of student cards. The trick is, though, to find out about all the little discounts that don't come to mind straight away.

For example, the bus company in your university town may offer special student tickets. I, in my days, could get a single ticket for 50p with my student card. Those who didn't know about the discount would pay the full fare without realising they're being ripped off!

Talking about public transport, you might also be able to get a young person's railcard. This comes really handy if you're planning to do lots of sightseeing during your time in the UK. Trains can be quite pricey but if you book in advance and use your railcard, you might be able to get some really good deals, including on first class tickets! So get yourself to a train station and get one whilst you can!

Lots of benefits come with a student card so make sure you always carry it around with you. For example, when you go shopping, it might be worth asking if they offer a student discount – you'll be surprised how many retailers do! If they don't, you can always look out for 'buy one get one free' deals, also known as BOGOF.

English

You're probably pretty good at English already if you're considering coming to study in the UK. However, to enable you to get even better, your university will most likely provide English language teaching services for international students. These can include, for example, academic writing classes, courses on giving presentations or general study skills.

It might be worth giving them a go. If you don't like them or think they're too easy, you can always give up.

Another important thing to remember, no matter how confident or not you feel about your English, is to always try to speak. Speak if you think you're good and if you think you're not good. Forget how you feel about your accent and what you think people might think about it. No one cares! Speak in seminars, join your university's debating society, chat to people when you go to a pub or a house party. It's the best way to master the language and gain some extra confidence. You'll be surprised how quickly you will pick up the little nuances and slang words that will make you sound more natural and fluent.

Speaking up is also something that university lecturers will appreciate. You're often marked on how much you contribute to seminars. So if you want to say something, say it before someone else does!

Speaking is also a great way to gain some extra confidence, which will give you an advantage in any future jobs or projects you might be involved in. So, don't be afraid – speak up!

Exams

The good news on this front is that not everyone has to take exams. Yes, you read that right – not every student in the UK has to take exams.

Everyone has to complete and submit some sort of coursework. However, whether or not you will need to take any exams will depend on the requirements of your particular course. My degree was English Literature and French. Throughout my time at university, I only had to take one written exam in English Literature – the rest was coursework, such as essays and other written assignments. These were marked the same way as exams so don't get too excited!

In French, on the other hand, I had so many exams I can't even count them now! Written, oral, formal, less formal – it was an exam extravaganza at my department.

A piece of advice here – I wouldn't recommend choosing a degree based on the number of exams you're required to sit. At the end of the day, you don't want to end up studying dance if you're a born architect, do you?

Another thing I thought I'd mention with regard to exams, which might seem obvious to most of you, is that cheating in any form is absolutely not allowed and not recommended. British universities take cheating very seriously – you can even get kicked out of your course. So please, please, please keep those elaborate mini-notes and internet-enabled devices out of the examination hall.

Freshers' week

Let's get things straight – freshers' week is not a week during which you eat fresh fruit and veg. Some might, in fact, argue that it's the very opposite!

Freshers' week is the week that comes directly before the start of the first term in your first year at university. Its primary purpose is to allow students to settle in, get over their homesickness and socialise with other first-years. There's also some formal stuff you may be required to do, such as registering for your course, with your university health service and the library, and buying all necessary textbooks.

Many universities organise freshers' fairs during their freshers' week. These are big fairs for first-year students during which societies, clubs and volunteering associations showcase what they do and recruit new members. You will be able to join your country's national society, or your university's international students' society, find out what sports are on offer at the university sports centre, where to have the tastiest and best-value lunch, and so on. Oh, and you'll get lots of freebies too! There will be plenty of free spatulas (weird, I know!), pens and badges on offer so make your way to the fair early and get your hands on them!

The end of freshers' week at many universities is marked with a freshers' ball. This is a grand event, especially if you like dressing up and drinking posh cocktails.

If you decide to skip your university's meet and greet, and orientation programmes, do not be tempted to also skip freshers' week. Freshers' week is when all the best fun happens!

Fry-up

Also known as the full English breakfast. This is something that you will hear about many a time. If you choose to stay in a student hall of residence, it's likely that a fry-up will be served for breakfast every Saturday. If not, your friends might suggest going out for a fry-up at a local cafe (not to be confused with a café, which is a place where non-authentic healthy-looking fry-ups tend to be served – you want the real thing, believe me).

A fry-up is made up of fried food, of course. Deep-fried food. Fried or scrambled eggs, bacon, sausages, tomatoes, mushrooms, hash browns – the list can go on and on. It's an essential part of student life because the greasiness of the fried food can perfectly soak up the alcohol consumed the night before. Or at least that's what we tell ourselves!

Funding

Funding is scarce but it does exist. Your university will definitely have a number of scholarships and bursaries that it will be happy to give to certain groups of students.

It might have very specific scholarships too. These are usually aimed at one or more particular groups within the student body. There might, for example, be a scholarship for female African students, or for students of geography whose research interests lie in a specific area of the subject.

It's good to find out about possible funding options well in advance. Your university's website will be a good starting point. And once you're there, you can speak to your personal tutor or departmental office. My main piece of advice would be to explore all options early and make sure your application is good!

Gap year

It's quite likely that during your first year at uni, you will hear people talk about their gap year. Make no mistake – they're not talking about a period of their life they can't remember. A gap year is a year between finishing college and going to university.

There are many different ways in which people spend their gap year, including getting a job, volunteering or working on a creative project of their own. However, the most common thing to do, by far, is to go 'travelling'.

When you hear a British person talk about 'travelling', you can be pretty certain that they don't mean going on a train up to Scotland. It's much more likely that they're talking about their gap year, which almost certainly involved travelling around the world. Asia, Australia, South America, and so on.

Graduation

Graduation might seem like a distant prospect for somebody who is only just starting university. However, it's good to know in advance what it's all about! It is a fun event and certainly unforgettable. And you will of course get to wear the famous hat and gown. You will also be able to take one of those cliché photos of you and your coursemates throwing your hats in the air. Well, it has to be done.

So, graduation is basically the formal ceremony during which students receive their degree certificates.

Do not be tempted to skip your graduation ceremony. Some international students might be tempted to do this because graduation ceremonies usually take place several weeks after the end of your course. By that time, the majority of UK students will have left the campus to go back to their hometown or move away to wherever they've found a job.

International students who decide to move back to their home country after graduating might think it's not worth going home and then travelling back to the UK for a weekend. However, you could plan it so that you can stay until the graduation weekend and go back to your country only after that. You could, for example, arrange to do a several-week-long internship or sign up for a volunteering scheme. Or you could get a temporary job at the university or somewhere in town. Or just go on holiday and come back to your university town to graduate!

Happy hour

A happy hour can be defined quite literally as an hour during which you're likely to be happy. That's not everything, though. A happy hour is a short period of time (usually two or three hours, in fact) during which you can buy cheap drinks in bars and pubs. Happy hours usually start before the evening rush, i.e. before most people head to the pubs. It's good to know when your local pub or university bar is doing a happy hour, especially if you want to try out some cocktails that would otherwise be too expensive to get when on a student budget.

Health

You might hear the phrase 'freshers' flu' being thrown around a lot. This is something that some people get. It's probably the exposure to so many new people, new food, new places, the sleepless nights, the drinks tasted, the food at university canteens, and other nasty things, that make some people feel feverish for a few days. This usually happens quite early on during the first term and supposedly only affects first-year students. Hence the term 'freshers' flu' (a 'fresher' is a student who has only just started university).

Don't worry, though – if you're feeling feverish, your university health service will be there to help. You will be asked to register with them as soon as you arrive at university, and you can then book an appointment when you need one. It might be worth checking whether your university requires a doctor's note if you miss a class due to feeling under the weather.

The university health service will also be able to provide you with information on sexual health and contraception (which is free of charge, by the way), and give you a sexual health check if you need one. So don't be embarrassed to ask them even the most embarrassing questions – they've heard it all before. And remember – it's better to be safe than sorry!

Internships

At some point during your degree, you are likely to hear about internships. Nowadays, more and more people apply to go to university, which means that there are lots of people to compete with for all the graduate jobs out there. Therefore, if you want to get a head start, think about doing an internship at some point during your course.

An internship is basically like having a job without really having a job. You will be working, your company will provide you with specific tasks or a project and you will, at last, have a chance to feel like a real adult.

Some companies will pay you – others will ask you to work for free. Either way – it's worth it. You'll get some proper work experience and a better idea of what jobs you want to be going for when you graduate. The commitment is often minimal too. You might be able to find a company or organisation that will be happy for you to come in just once or twice a week, or for a couple of weeks straight during the summer holidays. That way, you won't miss any of your lectures and you'll have some time to have fun too.

So, when you hear this word around, it will mean that everyone else is already thinking about doing it and you're lagging behind!

Journals

Libraries are not made up of books only. Books are just the visual side of things. It's all about the electronic journals. I didn't know about the existence of journals for a relatively long time but once I discovered them, I couldn't live without them anymore.

They are basically collections of academic essays written by researchers all over the world. They're more up to date than books because new essays are published in them regularly so you can stay be up to speed with all the recent developments in your area of research. And because they're electronic, they're so much easier to browse than books, which means you're going to be so much more productive!

Universities pay a fee for each journal their students are able to access. So make the most of them because that's what your own fees are going towards!

Lectures

Lectures are what differentiates school from university. They're serious classes for grown-ups. Unlike seminars, they are big-group classes – you can even get several hundred people attending one lecture.

Their purpose is essentially for a lecturer to provide a general outline of a topic, which you will later have an opportunity to discuss in small-group seminars. There aren't really many opportunities for discussion in lectures (unless you're having a Twitter discussion on your phone, hiding from the not so attentive eyes of your lecturer).

Left-hand traffic

Please, please, please remember to look the right way when crossing the road! And by 'the right way', I actually mean look right first. This is because Britain, unlike most countries in the world, has left-hand traffic.

Mature students

The definition of a mature student is not 'a student who is mature enough to avoid doing silly things at university'. Such people don't exist, and if they do – good for them!

A mature student, as defined by universities, is somebody who is aged 21 and over at the time of starting the first year of their undergraduate degree.

Most British people go to university straight after school or following their gap year. This is the case in most countries in the world, so I'm not saying anything that you wouldn't already know.

However, some people decide to start a degree several years after they've finished school. There are various reasons for this. For example, someone might have had a job for a few years but they decided that whatever they were doing was not for them and so applied to university to qualify to be a dentist. In this scenario, they are likely to be a mature student.

Meet and greet

By this point, you may have already received an international student's guide from the university you're applying to. It will most certainly mention 'meet and greet'. But do you know what they're talking about?

They actually want to meet and greet you straight after you get off your plane – isn't that nice? The organisers of your university's meet and greet scheme will arrange for a group of people to come and pick you up along with all the other international students landing at the same time. This is quite cool, to be honest with you. Especially if you have lots of luggage, laptop bags and so on. You won't get lost five times on the way from the airport to your halls/flat. You won't get lost even once! Signing up for a meet and greet is also a great way to meet some people that will be going to the same university.

A meet and greet scheme usually goes hand in hand with orientation.

Money

Make a budget. There are some brilliant apps around that allow you to enter your weekly budget and make it easier to stick to it.

If you're sharing accommodation with other students, it might be worth doing a big shop together and cooking for more people than just yourself. That way, you can save some money and you get the additional benefit of bonding with your flatmates over food!

If you have a part-time job, make sure you don't overpay tax. You may not need to pay any at all. For details, check Her Majesty's Revenue and Customs (HMRC) website.

If ever you run into financial difficulties, talk to someone. It could be your personal tutor or a students' union officer – they will definitely be able to give you some tips and advice, or direct you towards the right people.

If your budget is tight, think about applying for funding as well.

Nightlife

Student life in the UK is, to a great extent, about going out. Nightlife in many university towns is geared up for students. There are student nights out in local bars and clubs, and student deals. There are gigs and themed nights out, and fancy dress parties. Make the most of them!

National Union of Students

The National Union of Students (NUS) is a national association that represents the student body, campaigns on its behalf, and defends and promotes students' rights. It unites the individual students' unions around the UK and supports their work. It's what a central government is to local governments, if you're still not sure what I'm talking about.

The NUS is a big thing and its importance within the UK student life should not be underestimated. It's not like a student council – it's way more serious than that.

Whoever becomes the president of the NUS stands a good chance of getting into serious politics, if not becoming a prime minister. Many high-profile British politicians and business people started off as NUS presidents, and – before that – presidents of their university's students' union. So if you're up for a career in politics, or if you just want to improve your job prospects, it might be worth considering starting your campaign on day one of your time at university.

Orientation

Orientation is something that usually goes with a 'meet and greet'.

Orientation is not the same as orienteering (an activity that involves using a map and compass to navigate from one point to another) – don't get the two terms mixed up (both of them are big university things). Orientation is a social programme, designed mainly for international students, which helps them get used to the way things are in the UK and in their university town before the start of the first term.

It usually lasts for a week or longer. It's basically like being on holiday with like-minded people. It's fun. You usually stay in a university hall of residence with other newly arrived international students and a team of facilitators employed by the university. These guys are usually current or former students – they know their stuff. They are there to help you out with everything – from explaining how to use the old-fashioned English taps (one for cold water and one for hot water – weird but true) to finding the best lunch place on campus, or guiding you through the dos and don'ts of freshers' week. They also run lots of organised activities throughout the day for the duration of the orientation programme. These may include a tour around your university library, a trip to the city centre or purely social activities like a pub quiz or a sporting event.

People who do orientation together usually stay friends with a lot of the other participants throughout their university time. However, there can be drawbacks to this. If you make lots of friends among international students, you may not feel the need or make an effort to meet home students, or those who didn't sign up for orientation. When you're an international student in the UK, one of the fun bits is getting to know the local culture and people. Therefore, make sure that you also hang out with the Brits from your course or the residence you're staying at. They'll be happy to get to know you too!

Personal tutors

At most universities, each student is assigned to a member of staff within their university department. It is usually somebody who teaches one of the compulsory modules you need to attend in your first year.

The role of a personal tutor is to provide academic and pastoral support to individual students. In your first year, this will usually involve checking on how well you're settling in, how you're getting on with your coursework, whether you're getting on with your flatmates and coursemates, and so on. They will also look at your grades throughout your degree and offer support where you need it. They will then provide you with guidance on writing your dissertation or a covering letter for jobs you will be applying for.

Personal tutors – despite what the term may suggest – do not provide one-to-one tuition. You will be taught in a class with other students – you can, however, arrange to meet them to discuss anything you're unsure about with regard to coursework or any other topic.

Politics

Some students at British universities are politically active. It doesn't necessarily mean that they are members of political parties, although some might be. Universities provide plenty of opportunities for students to get involved in politics, including societies and debating clubs. Some even make their premises available for external organisations to meet and discuss politics.

These political groups' activities may include campaigning against rising tuition fees, against climate change, or for equal rights of all within the student body. Others also extend their activities beyond the university and aim to tackle bigger national, and even international issues.

Many international students find it interesting to get to know the British political system and get involved in various campaigns at a local level. So if this is something you're interested in, make your way to your university's freshers' fair and explore what's happening on your campus.

Rag week

Rag societies are student organisations whose principal aim is to raise money for various charitable causes.

Many of them are active all year round – others only during the 'rag week', which is one week each year when lots of fundraising activities take place every day.

Rag might be something that you may want to join if you want to work in the charitable sector once you've graduated. Even if you don't, however, it's a great thing to be involved in because it raises money for so many great causes!

Reading week

That's technically a week during which you're supposed to work, work and work. It's free of classes and other compulsory activities taking place at university. It's supposed to be time that you get to take a step back, think about where you are with your coursework and then get on with the work. You might have lots of stuff to read, or an essay to write. You might be asked to think about your dissertation topic when you're in your final year.

I said 'you're supposed to', because in practice, reading weeks tend to be slightly different than in theory. Many people do indeed catch up on their academic studies and spend hours in the library. However, it's also a time when they socialise with their friends or go away for a couple of days – either to visit their family home or take a trip with their friends.

Make sure, however, that the idea of a free week doesn't tempt you to party too hard, though. It's all about reading in the end – so do get on with it!

Seminars

These are small-group classes which are more practical than lectures. They usually involve hands-on activities or a discussion of a specific topic that was referred to during a lecture.

Seminars are usually quite interactive and you're usually asked to prepare for them in advance so that you can participate fully and make the most of them.

Slang

'You're alright?', 'You alright?' or simply 'Alright?' means 'How is it going?' or 'How are you?'. It's a normal conversation starter. It doesn't mean that people think there's something wrong with you, which is exactly what I thought when I first heard it. I thought I either look like I'm lost, scared or have something on my face, which I'm not aware of. Well, it took me a while to work this one out, but once I did, I started to use the phrase myself, which made me sound more natural and friendly.

Other words you might want to know before you go to the UK include 'ta' and 'cheers' (which both mean 'thank you').

People will also call you 'mate', 'man', 'dude', 'love', 'dear' and 'duck', depending on which area of the UK you're in and who you're talking to.

I wouldn't recommend using slang until you feel perfectly confident that you know what you're doing. Once you do, start using it or otherwise, you might end up sounding like you're taking yourself a little bit too seriously!

Societies

Societies are organised groups of students who are interested in a particular activity. For example, there might be an arts society at your university. This is just a group of students who get together every week or so and talk about art, do art together or go and visit art galleries. They might organise their own nights out where they party together, or big parties where they socialise with members of other societies.

One idea for an international student is to join their country's society or an international students' society. These usually hold lots of international parties where you can socialise with other international students, eat lots of international food and generally have a good time.

Sport

Universities are very, very good with sports. Most universities will have a number of sports clubs that you can join, and a wide range of sports on offer. Tennis, rugby, football, swimming – these are just examples.

Many universities also have subsidised gyms where you can get a monthly or annual membership and go as much as you like.

Some things to remember: rugby league and rugby union are actually two different sports, a cricket game can go on all day (and beyond) so don't make a commitment unless you know what you're getting into, football is like a religion in the UK, and nobody really cares about volleyball, basketball or handball.

Student common room

This is where all the cool kids hang out. Or maybe it's the opposite! Anyway, this is where I used to hang out in my first weeks at my university – a great place to have a chat to people who live in your halls, are doing the same course as you, or just friendly-looking faces.

A student common room is usually located in student halls of residence, a students' union building or a university department. It's 'common' because everyone is entitled to use it, as long as they're using it reasonably. I'm saying reasonably because not everyone goes there to have a chat – some people might actually be there to do some serious work!

Others will have lunch there. Depending on what your food smells like, you may be welcome to have it there, or the very opposite!

Sometimes, student common rooms are used for various functions. During a students' union election, for example, they may be used as rooms where students cast their votes. A student common room could also be used for a party run by your university's international students' society. So keep an eye out for those – some interesting stuff might be happening just around the corner.

Student loan

This is something that a lot of British, and indeed European Union students will be talking about a lot. You may already be aware that the UK (and especially English) university system is only partly funded by the government. A big chunk of the total cost has to be covered by the students themselves, and that's where student loans come in.

Student loans are not just there to pay for university fees but also all the other goods (read: leisure activities) that come with student life. The loan is paid in installments. Therefore, you should be aware that if you're asking somebody out just before the next instalment is due, they might say no, and they're not saying no because they don't want to hang out with you, but because they need the cash to hang out with you.

Students' union

Each university will have its own slang and jargon, but the students' union exists pretty much everywhere. People meet up at the union, people go to union events, have lunch at the union and sign up for volunteering at the union's volunteering office. It's basically the place to be.

The union is technically an association of offices that run student life.

The students' union in Sheffield, which is where I went to university, was a building but also a world of its own. It was the focal point of student life, a place where you could find out what's on and take part in it. There were hundreds of activities on offer each week – anything from bouldering and hiking, to contemporary dance and theatre, to science clubs and photography classes. You could learn how to make jewellery, go on a kayaking trip, have a go at learning Arabic or join an animal protection society. These are just examples, and at most universities there's something for everyone.

When you're new to a place, it's very easy to stay in your comfort zone, so make sure you try as many new things that your union has on offer as possible. You never know – you might discover a new passion!

Study abroad

I know – you didn't come to the UK to then go off to another country. But being an international student doesn't prevent you from exploring the option of spending a semester or even a year at another university abroad. Most universities run student exchange programmes, which might be very beneficial for your personal development and future career prospects.

Even if you don't speak another language (in addition to English and your native tongue), you should consider giving it a go. Most foreign universities that British universities partner with run courses for international students which are taught and assessed in English.

If you do want to give it a go, make sure you submit your application early – speak to your personal tutor about deadlines in your department.

Tap water

One mistake that many visitors to the UK make is paying for drinking water. In many countries, you need to pay for a bottle of mineral water with your meal, but in the UK water is free!

So next time you're having a meal with friends, just ask for a jug of tap water to share. It comes directly from the tap and is safe to drink. It might taste differently in different cities but this does not affect quality.

It's also useful to know that you can ask for a pint of tap water in a pub. This will help you stay hydrated and avoid those terrible hangovers!

Tea

It's drunk with milk. That's how you should make it for other people and that's how they will make it for you when you ask for some. With regard to preparation techniques – there's a milk-first/tea-first divide when deciding what goes in the cup first. Watch the pros and soon you'll know how to make a perfect cuppa.

In the north of England, tea may also mean dinner. This is slightly confusing. If you're inviting a southern person for tea – they will expect a hot beverage. A northerner might take it for an invitation to a full-blown food feast. So be careful and set your expectations clearly!

Uni

Nobody will really call it university. Apart from your parents and grandparents probably. It's uni. You're going to uni. You're at uni. You're doing uni coursework. Your uni friends this and that. This is something that you will probably pick up once you've been in the UK for a while. But please, don't call it university in your final year. You should probably only call it that once you've been in a serious job for a few years.

Volunteering

Volunteering is very popular at British universities. It's generally quite an integral part of British life.

Volunteering is an altruistic activity which aims to improve the quality of life for other people and animals, or improve a community or environment. It can be, for example, promoting your local theatre, teaching a foreign language to members of your local community, cooking meals for homeless people or looking after a public garden.

Most universities will have a volunteering office that offers volunteering vacancies at various organisations. Some of them get filled up fast so make sure you put your name down quickly – otherwise someone else will!

If you're interested in volunteering, you may also want to get involved in your university's rag society, or help organise their rag week.

Weather

The final thing that you must remember, and I've already said it in the introduction to this guide, is that bad weather is not a good enough excuse for a British student to stay in. Weather is unpredictable in most areas of the UK, and relying on weather forecasts is probably not a good idea. If you don't like going out when it rains, you might end up spending days on end staying in (missing lectures and missing out on student life!). So get some wellies, a rain coat or an umbrella and go out and have fun!

Thanks for reading!

For further information about studying in the UK, including videos with general learning tips, have a look at my blog:

www.ukstudentlifeguide.wordpress.com

NOTES

Printed in Great Britain
by Amazon.co.uk, Ltd.,
Marston Gate.